Congregations,
Neighborhoods,
Places

CALVIN SHORTS

Congregations, Neighborhoods, Places

by Mark T. Mulder

CALVIN SHORTS

Calvin PRESS

COLLEGE

Grand Rapids, MI • calvin.edu/press

Published 2018 by the Calvin College Press
3201 Burton St. SE
Grand Rapids, MI 49546

Publisher's Cataloging-in-Publication data
Names: Mulder, Mark T., author.
Title: Congregations , neighborhoods , places / Mark T. Mulder.
Series: Calvin Shorts.
Description: Includes bibliographical references. | Grand Rapids, MI : Calvin College Press, 2018.
Identifiers: ISBN 978-1-937555-28-3 (pbk.) | 978-1-937555-29-0 (ebook) | LCCN 2018930645
Subjects: LCSH Communities--Religious aspects--Christianity. | Mission of the church. | Church work. | Christian sociology--United States. | Religion and sociology. | Community development, Urban--United States. | Church and social problems--United States. | Community leadership--United States. | Faith-based human services--United States. | BISAC RELIGION / Christian Life / Social Issues | SOCIAL SCIENCE / Sociology of Religion | SOCIAL SCIENCE / Sociology / Urban
Classification: LCC BV625 .M84 2018 | DDC 253--dc23

Cover design: Robert Alderink
Interior design and typeset: Katherine Lloyd, The DESK

Contents

Acknowledgements

This book's origins can be traced to the June 2016 Writers' Co-op at Calvin College. That week of dedicated writing within a community of scholars afforded a nurturing environment to begin expanding on the ideas that appear in the pages that follow. I am grateful to the Calvin Center for Christian Scholarship and the Calvin Institute of Christian Worship for their financial support of this project during the Co-op and after. I also extend my gratitude to Susan Felch and Dale Williams for their careful oversight of the manuscript. Michael Emerson's close reading of an earlier draft has significantly improved this little book, and I offer my profound appreciation. My thanks as well to the deacons of Sherman Street Christian Reformed Church—their faithfulness and integrity are an inspiration.

Congregations, Neighborhoods, Places **is underwritten by the Calvin Institute of Christian Worship and the Calvin Center for Christian Scholarship.**

Series Editor's Foreword

Midway along the journey of our life
I woke to find myself in some dark woods,
For I had wandered off from the straight path.

So begins the *Divine Comedy*, a classic meditation on the Christian life, written by Dante Alighieri in the fourteenth century.

Dante's three images—a journey, a dark forest, and a perplexed pilgrim—still feel familiar today, don't they?

We can readily imagine our own lives as a series of journeys, not just the big journey from birth to death, but also all the little trips from home to school, from school to job, from place to place, from old friends to new. In fact, we often feel we are simultaneously on multiple journeys that tug us in diverse and sometimes opposing directions. We recognize those dark woods from fairy tales and nightmares and the all-too-real conundrums that crowd our everyday lives. No wonder we frequently feel perplexed. We wake up shaking our heads, unsure if we know how to live wisely today or tomorrow or next week.

This series has in mind just such perplexed pilgrims. Each book invites you, the reader, to walk alongside experienced guides who will help you understand the contours of the road as well as the surrounding landscape. They will cut back the underbrush, untangle myths and misconceptions, and suggest ways to move forward.

And they will do it in books intended to be read in an evening or during a flight. Calvin Shorts are designed not just for perplexed pilgrims, but also for busy ones. We live in a complex and changing world. We need nimble ways to acquire knowledge, skills, and wisdom. These books are one way to meet those needs.

John Calvin, after whom this series is named, recognized our pilgrim condition. "We are always on the road," he said, and although this road, this life, is full of perplexities, it is also "a gift of divine kindness which is not to be refused." Calvin Shorts takes as its starting point this claim that we are called to live well in a world that is both gift and challenge.

In the *Divine Comedy*, Dante's guide is Virgil, a wise but not omniscient mentor. So too, the authors in the Calvin Shorts series don't pretend to know it all. They, like you and me, are pilgrims. And they invite us to walk with them as together we seek to live more faithfully in this world that belongs to God.

Susan M. Felch
Executive Editor
The Calvin College Press

Additional Resources

Additional online resources for *Congregations, Neighborhoods, Places* may be available at www.calvin.edu/press.

Additional information, references, and citations are included in the notes at the end of this book. Rather than using footnote numbers, these comments are keyed to phrases and page numbers.

Churches
as Neighbors

THE OVERNIGHTERS

How hard is it to be a good neighbor? If we think about chatting over a backyard fence, or taking cookies to a new mom, or saying "hi" to the kids next-door when they get off the school bus, the answer may be "not very hard." But when we think deeply about being good neighbors, we quickly realize there is more to it than these pleasant encounters.

When Jesus talked with a lawyer about being a good neighbor, his standard was high: love God and love your neighbor as yourself (Luke 10:25-28). And then Jesus made it more difficult. When the lawyer asked, "Who is my neighbor?" Jesus told a story about a good Samaritan (Luke 10:30-37). This story spins neighborliness out to include foreigners and people we don't like and includes issues of violence, justice, and the need for safe places, like the inn where the Samaritan takes the wounded man. To be a good neighbor turns out to be rather complicated and difficult.

The early church understood the seriousness of being a good neighbor. For instance, it encouraged members to sell their property to care for those in need (Acts 2:44-45). Taking care of the widowed, the sick, and the poor were not simply a few activities among others. Rather, they became a hallmark of the ancient church. Later leaders like John Chrysostom made bold declarations on the subject: "It is foolishness and a public madness to fill the cupboards with clothing and allow men who are created in God's image and likeness to stand naked and trembling with the cold so that they can hardly hold themselves upright." Chrysostom understood that it is not enough merely to be kind or to help a few individuals. Caring for neighbors requires a robust commitment. Neighborliness is an ongoing community responsibility. In fact, a church that doesn't care for its neighbors commits a "public madness."

This challenge to our churches remains today. When we expand "neighbor" to "neighborhoods" and when we move from merely being nice to our next-door neighbor to thinking about creating better neighborhoods, we find that being a good neighbor is harder than we thought. If we add to the mix not just the street where we live but also the streets around our churches, the problems—and the opportunities—multiply. What does it mean not only for us as individuals but also for our congregations to be good neighbors to our community? How do we avoid falling into "a public madness?"

The 2014 documentary film *The Overnighters* tries to answer these questions. At the very least, it shows us how complex the questions are. The film is set in Williston, North Dakota, a small rural town with fewer than 15,000 people, 93 percent of them white. Then in the early 2000s at the nearby Bakken Shield, oil was discovered. Suddenly there were jobs, lots of jobs, and men looking for work poured into town. Williston's population doubled. For a time, rents were higher in Williston than anywhere else in the country. But even if men could pay the high rents, there was still a problem. Williston simply could not accommodate so many people. The men who found jobs literally had no place to stay.

Enter the star of the movie, Jay Reinke, the pastor of a Lutheran church in Williston. Pastor Reinke sees that these desperate men need shelter. So he opens up his entire church—from sanctuary to parking lot—as a place of refuge for anyone in need, and the men are grateful. But the church members begin to worry. This is *their* church, they think. Does the pastor have the right to hand it over to outsiders? They wonder about the criminal backgrounds of some of the new tenants. They become defensive and suspicious, and then they organize to keep the oilfield employees off church grounds.

Though the film includes a complicated third act, *The Overnighters* displays some of the best and worst elements in churches and how they relate to their neighborhoods. First is the local need: lack of housing. Second, the pastor realizes that the church has space that remains unused overnight. Third, the pastor uses the resources of the church to meet a community-wide need. However, the church members have different ideas about proper uses of the church. They question whether it should be used to house transient oilfield employees. They have real concerns but also real prejudices, and the film helps us understand how complex it can be for a church to be a good neighbor.

In *The Overnighters*, we see a picture of the failures of local congregations, but also the possibilities. The pastor wanted to use congregational resources to minister to some of the "least of these." In fact, as the church members feared, many of the oilfield workers did have criminal records and could get work nowhere else. Even with a job, they could not afford the high rents in Williston. The pastor and the Lutheran church became their housing salvation. On the other hand, many congregational members saw the church as "theirs" and had little interest in sharing their building and their parking lot. They also had legitimate concerns about issues of safety. The film itself does not necessarily resolve these issues well, but it does offer a vivid example of what being a good neighbor could involve for a church.

CHURCHES AND THEIR LOCAL NEIGHBORHOODS

The Overnighters raises this query: How should congregations engage their neighborhoods? This is a question that churches in many different traditions are asking. In recent decades, more churches have decided that they want to be "missional." That is, they see themselves as missionaries in their own neighborhoods. They want to reach people who are outside the congregation. In many cases, that outreach includes social service programs. However, churches don't necessarily know how to design good social service programs. A number of experts have recently argued that often these neighborhood engagement programs actually do more harm than good. So what is a church to do?

This book is an attempt to think with congregations, particularly congregations in cities, about how social science might help them become better neighbors. Social science can both help churches become more aware of themselves and of those who live around them. When churches better understand who they are and what their neighborhood is like, they can more effectively become good neighbors.

And neighborhoods matter dearly. The nature and structure of a neighborhood and the opportunities it offers or withholds affects everyone who lives there. A neighborhood can provide a sense of well-being or of threat. The nature of the neighborhood creates the social environment, level of public safety, and quality of public services that the people who live there experience. The demographics of the neighborhood determines who will be peers at school and the types of networks those school-children will develop, both personally and professionally. In fact, a neighborhood has so much influence, some people argue that "a person's life chances can be statistically explained by their zip code." To some extent, we could say that we all grow up with "zip code destinies."

I am a social scientist and a church member. I have studied a good many churches and neighborhoods, and I recognize the complexities described in *The Overnighters*. My hope is that this little book can help us think about these complexities so that our congregations can become better neighbors. We should appreciate the true and even radical gifts that churches bring to their neighborhoods. But we should also become more reflective about the best ways to engage our local communities.

In the second chapter, we will look at how churches are perceived and how they actually function in local communities. In the third and fourth chapters, we will discuss all the good work that congregations can offer and at the same time recognize the challenges and limitations that churches face. Chapters five, six, and seven suggest paths forward for congregations—recognizing existing church resources, addressing both individual and systemic issues, and cooperating with other congregations. Finally, in the eighth chapter, I will encourage churches to build on their own histories of caring.

Churches—
What We See
and What is Real

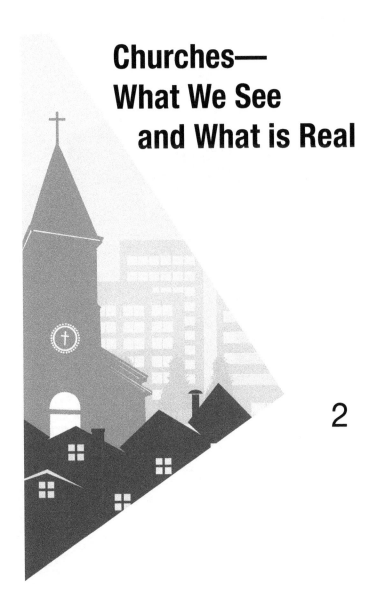

2

COMPETING PERCEPTIONS AND REALITIES

Will is a twenty-five-year-old barista in a Great Lakes city. He grew up in a family who attended church every week, but now he has become disillusioned and "bored" with organized religion. While he acknowledges that he still "feels" like he believes, Will has no interest in sitting in pews with "hypocrites who don't seem to reflect the love and generosity of Jesus." In short, Will represents a growing percentage of Americans who feel that churches no longer have much to offer in solving social problems.

Despite this rising sentiment about churches in general, the new arrivals in the rural town of Williston in the movie *The Overnighters*, discussed in chapter 1, experienced something different. They relied on the Lutheran church as a place of refuge. Congregations in city centers can play similar vital roles in their communities. In some cases, city churches are already valued for their contributions to their neighborhoods. In other cases, however, critics like Will see them as full of hypocrisy and self-interest. These competing perceptions point to real issues within and among churches.

Churches can powerfully influence their communities for the good. A case from Wisconsin proves this point. For the last twelve years, the mayor of Milwaukee, Tom

Barret, has instituted a "Ceasefire Sabbath." On this desig-
nated Sunday, he visits various churches to appeal for an
end to gun violence and for improved public safety in the
city. In these speeches, Barret stresses his own responsibility as a public leader. However, he also notes that these
faith-based organizations reach people that he cannot.
He comes for a day. Churches live week by week in their
communities. Churches can work on a regular basis to
improve safety within their neighborhoods, and he urges
them to do so. With "Ceasefire Sabbath," we see a unique
role that churches *might* play in cities.

We know that when churches show interest in community issues, those outside the church find the church
to be more attractive. For instance, Latino Protestant
churches have been growing rapidly in the United States.
At least some of this growth is due to their active community engagement. Research shows that some Latinos move
from Catholic to Protestant churches in part because they
perceive that Protestant churches are more engaged with
their neighborhoods. They also think that Protestant
churches will help them develop their leadership potential.

Congregations tend to act as hubs for many Latino Protestants. At least part of the reason churches are central is that
Latino Protestants suffer from a "double marginalization."
They exist as a religious minority (most Latinos are Catholic) within a racial minority (most people in the United
States are not Latino). As a result, their congregations necessarily become both refuges and sites of public action and

advocacy. One study of Latino churches in Chicago compared Protestant and Catholic congregations. They found that some Latinos preferred Protestant churches because they offered more opportunities to learn civic skills. These skills, in turn, led to higher levels of civic engagement.

In other words, Latino Protestant congregations, to varying degrees, seem to foster civic engagement and leadership opportunities. And they do this for a population that has been historically marginalized. They also provide both material and social services. Elizabeth Dias, a *Time* magazine journalist, notes that many Latino Protestant churches become "de facto healing centers for a population with limited health care benefits. They act as food banks for people with empty refrigerators. They house people avoiding street violence. There's a lot more going on there than just saving souls." These Latino Protestant congregations serve as a model of how churches may become sites of community engagement and social services.

On the other hand, not all city churches are socially engaged. Some churches seem impotent and selfish. Many studies show that more and more people in the United States have grown disillusioned with churches. In turn, church and religious leaders have voiced concern about the growing percentage of "nones." "Nones" are individuals, like Will, who claim no religious affiliation. Some interpret the growth of the "nones" as a sign that the United States has finally become a secular nation. Closer study, though, reveals that the "nones" see themselves less as unbelievers and more as disaffiliated. In other words, the "nones" are disenchanted with the church. But they do not necessarily reject all religious belief.

Thus, even self-identified "believers" may be skeptical of the church. Recent surveys report that a shrinking percentage of people say that churches contribute to solving important social problems. In 2009, 75 percent said that houses of worship offered solutions to social ills. In 2016, only 56 percent agreed. At the same time, the percentage who said that churches had little or nothing to offer grew from 23 percent to 39 percent. It seems communities of faith could use an image consultant when it comes to their role in addressing social concerns.

WHAT CHURCHES DO WELL

We should take this negative evidence seriously, but sometimes churches get a bad rap. While congregations may at times be preoccupied with themselves, it is rarely true that they just ignore their neighborhoods. I have conducted nearly four hundred interviews with attenders of Latino Protestant, Catholic, mainline, evangelical, and African-American Protestant churches. In these interviews, most congregants expressed a strong desire to engage their communities. Other researchers have confirmed these findings. In fact, some have described church community engagement as so widespread in the United States that it is best described as a *congregational norm*. Both congregational leaders and members expect active involvement in their neighborhoods as simply a matter of course. Moreover, people in need assume that aid from congregations is natural and normal. We might even say that receiving aid from a local church is considered to be part of the "natural order" of society. Because churches are a stable presence, many have earned large amounts of trust and legitimacy in their neighborhoods.

Not only do congregations expect to be involved, but most congregations *want* to be involved in their communities. They see neighborhood participation as a natural outgrowth of their mission. They would agree with Chrysostom that ignoring their neighbors is "foolishness and a public madness." Congregational social activity also tends to spur other action. Individuals who attend churches that have a strong and clear priority on community care are, in turn, more likely than other people to be civically engaged outside the congregation. In other words, congregational activity has ripple effects.

For example, Carlos and Juanita Garcia attend their local church, Alabanza, nearly every week, missing only on occasion. They not only attend worship but also serve in their church. Carlos teaches the second graders, and Juanita helps run their church's food pantry. In addition, they both volunteer in a local homeless shelter.

It turns out that going to church weekly—like the Garcias—actually leads to more volunteering, not just in the church but also in the larger community. Political scientists report that more Americans are involved in a religious organization than in any other type of association, group, or club. And these Americans are good volunteers. One study found that compared to a typical once-a-year churchgoer, the average weekly churchgoer volunteers many more hours—an extra 10.5 hours a month for religious causes and an extra 6.4 hours a month for secular causes. Thus, we see that congregations are often places where individuals and families *learn* to engage the larger society.

I have discovered from interviews that most churches, especially city churches, make community engagement one of their priorities. In some instances, congregations encourage their members to relocate to the church's neighborhood. This allows more people to offer intense, local commitment. One member of an urban evangelical church told me, "People have moved into the neighborhood from the suburbs to help."

Some churches look carefully at the needs in their local area. Then they develop various kinds of services to respond to these perceived needs. One member of an urban evangelical congregation described his church's relationship to its neighborhood this way, "[My church] is trying to get pretty involved. We do tutoring with the kids right in [the local apartment complex]. We do ESL with the people right around [the church]. . . . We also have a food pantry so local people can come by."

Whether mainline, evangelical, Catholic, Latino Protestant, or African-American Protestant—all the congregations I have interviewed report church activities in their neighborhoods. They engage with their local communities, and they do it regularly. Church members from a variety of theological, racial, and geographic backgrounds think that churches, as a matter of course, should meet needs in their own neighborhoods. When interviewed, they rarely acknowledge that these services are atypical or unexpected. Most, in fact, tend to speak rather matter-of-factly.

The following statement from a man who attends a suburban evangelical church is fairly typical: "Our mission is about announcing God's kingdom through missional communities for the oppressed. And I realize 'the oppressed' is sort of a weighty term that carries with it all kinds of things, and you can get into all kinds of conversations about whether or not it's the appropriate term. But . . . we've committed to partnering with the City of Grand Rapids to end homelessness." For this member, it was the church's own mission that led to service. In other words, to avoid "public madness," the church *had* to work with those who are oppressed or marginalized. This engagement is simply the church doing the business of the church.

CONCLUSION

Most churches tend to take community engagement seriously. Some people think that congregations are only interested in themselves, but for the most part this is simply not true. However, wanting to be active in the community and being effectively active are two different things. Churches interested in community engagement should learn to *accurately* assess both their limits and capacities. Issues of inequality and disadvantage are complex. Good intentions are not enough. For example, social science research is quite clear that poverty has deep structural foundations. Moreover, poverty looks different in different places. Because of these complexities, there exists no step-by-step formula for congregational engagement to alleviate poverty that simply translates to all communities or neighborhoods. Instead, church leaders should be encouraged to *first* deeply study and understand their own context. A key step in that process is to consider what the characteristics of a congregation actually are and what they might do well.

What
Congregations
Do Well

3

WHAT IS A CONGREGATION?

On a rainy Sunday morning in March, I visited a small Latino congregation, Community Presbyterian. They met in a modest brick building outside the Fruitvale neighborhood of Oakland, California. During the service, the pastor lamented that members have been forced to commute to church from long distances. Though he did not use the word "gentrification," it was clear that rising real estate prices in the Bay Area were squeezing the housing options for the congregation. In response to these increasing prices, Community Presbyterian has begun a program that offers legal advice for those who face rent-hiking landlords. The church also helps to identify affordable housing options in the city. In addition, Community Presbyterian offers computer-training classes, ESL classes, and immigration status services.

Churches like Community Presbyterian tend to be busy places. They have a wide range of activities and rhythms. These activities and rhythms are so familiar, however, that most church members don't spend much time reflecting on who their congregation is and what it does. So we begin this chapter with a definition of "congregation."

A "congregation" is a group of people who gather at regularly scheduled times in a particular place for worship.

If we break that definition apart, we find that congregations meet several expectations: 1) They find unity in a common religious belief. 2) They meet regularly. 3) They meet in a specific location. 4) They maintain a voluntary membership. 5) They recognize some type of formalized leadership. 6) They have a formal name and identity that marks them as different from other congregations.

Congregations also possess certain features that allow them to actually get work done. First, congregations rely on volunteer labor. Of course, many nonprofits also rely on volunteer labor. Congregations, though, do so to a much greater degree than any other similar organization. To be sure, most churches also have paid staff who provide professional leadership. But they typically depend on the countless hours of volunteers who donate time, energy, and even expertise. These donations make congregations both stable and vital members of the community.

Second, congregations have built-in practices and routines. Think for a moment about just the worship services. As the centerpiece of congregational life, the worship services demand ongoing planning and work. Although much of this activity occurs behind the scenes, reflect on the amount of work a worship service requires. Each week a sermon is prepared. Music is chosen and practiced. Bulletins are typed and printed. Wine or juice and bread are purchased at the store and prepared for communion. After most of the people have left, the sanctuary, foyer, and bathrooms are cleaned. And these are just a few of the weekly tasks. Churches are little volunteer schools. The worship services alone allow congregations to practice and refine volunteer work. In short, churches require so much volunteer work that they necessarily become masters of it.

Third, congregations are different from other nonprofit organizations. They have the unique feature of longevity. They stick around for a while. Other types of nonprofit organizations tend to come and go. They lack the ability to outlast changes in needs, social climate, and the economy. For example, some research has focused on churches that remain in neighborhoods that have lost their economic vitality. These churches continue to offer support to a community in distress. A new congregation is vulnerable and can dissolve quite easily. But compared to both for-profit and nonprofit organizations, once a church reaches a level of stability, it has a better chance of surviving for a long time.

CHURCHES AS SIGNIFICANT CITY INSTITUTIONS

Churches are stable organizations that can be found in nearly every neighborhood. But they are not always taken seriously as important city institutions. (We usually define institutions as organizations that have profound and long-lasting influence.) For example, a recent twenty-five-year study in Baltimore examined the lives of poor urban youth as they grew and became adults. The researchers looked at family background, work opportunities, neighborhood context, race, gender, and schools. In short, they thoroughly examined the legacy of poverty from many points of view. However, they failed to mention a key institution in many city neighborhoods: *churches*. Such an oversight, unfortunately, is fairly common.

Another recent book about the South Side of Chicago looks at the negative effects of extreme residential segregation. The book cover actually features a photograph of an iconic urban church steeple. Yet the author ignored actual churches and offered no insights into how the churches in these neighborhoods engaged with issues of racial segregation. These oversights are strange because many studies have shown that churches are the most widespread community organizations in the United States. Clearly, to fully account for neighborhoods, the role of churches must be understood. Some congregations might remain passive about issues of inequality, especially when their neighborhoods change. But others have actively helped their communities restructure. Unfortunately, researchers often underestimate the role that congregations play in shaping urban contexts.

That these important studies ignore congregations raises two questions. First, are these analyses correct when they implicitly dismiss churches as agents of community change? That question can be easily answered with a "no." Other research has clearly shown that churches have rich social capital and deliver a large amount of social services.

That is, they help to create networks and relationships marked by trust and cooperation while providing services that nurture stronger communities. Some scholars even insist that churches offer the best hope for cities. Manufacturing jobs and white middle class families fled the cities in the last half of the twentieth century. But many churches stayed. These churches remain as one of the few institutions in these forgotten neighborhoods with enough presence to renew the "cultural, moral, economic, and political life of the cities." That raises the second question. What might these faith communities actually *do* in their neighborhoods to be forces of positive change?

THE ECONOMIC BENEFITS OF CHURCHES

So what do churches contribute to their neighborhoods? They contribute volunteer time. But they also contribute real economic benefits. As we saw in chapter 2, few congregations simply focus on themselves and ignore the neighborhoods around them. In fact, the vast majority actually provide social services for their neighborhoods, whether they label them as such or not. For instance, a 2006 study of 1,400 Philadelphia congregations found that *every* one of them provided some type of social service. A similar study in Kent County, Michigan, found that the churches generated between $95 and $118 million annually in "in-kind" serving ministries. "In-kind" refers to services and items that are donated. These ministries ranged from counseling to food pantries to emergency financial assistance to job placement to housing, and much more. The study also found that churches provided over 2,800 volunteers annually for education programs alone.

My own research in Grand Rapids, Michigan, has revealed that many churches actively seek to be involved, but not necessarily in their own neighborhood. During interviews, some church members said they didn't provide social services or community activities. But they frequently named ministries that the church supported in the region. Sometimes a congregation thinks that its immediate surrounding area has plenty of material or spiritual resources, which then frees them up to focus on areas that are perceived to have greater needs, such as the core city. Or the church may participate in larger programs that serve the metropolitan area. As a man attending a suburban evangelical church told me: "Most of the programs we run are for the less fortunate communities downtown in the inner city of Grand Rapids. So we don't really talk about the community the church is located in."

Congregations often begin to target other areas for ministry when they, rightly or wrongly, perceive that the area around the church does not need any type of aid. I discovered a similar case when I spoke to a suburban Catholic parishioner about his congregation's interactions with neighbors. He described a missional presence that focused on the core city: "[Our church does] a lot of projects, not necessarily in [the suburb], but around Grand Rapids. So [church members] don't necessarily have interaction with the people of [the suburb]. But where work needs to be done in Grand Rapids, they tend to go to those places."

In other words, these interviews revealed that it is a congregational norm to provide social and community services. If congregations think that the area surrounding their church doesn't need their help, they actively look for another venue. Local congregations can be so dynamic that some studies have found that they frequently provide an informal social safety net.

These findings are not unique to the United States. A Canadian study reported that just among twelve Toronto congregations, the accumulated economic contribution of the churches to the city came to an annual average value of $4,320,848 per congregation. Even smaller congregations had impacts that seem to outweigh their size. A Presbyterian church included in the study had only 150 members and an annual budget of about $260,000. But the authors of the study estimated that the church's economic contribution likely approached $1.5 million every year. Because of these impressive social and economic contributions, some researchers describe congregations as having social and economic "Halo Effects" in their communities. The findings challenge the notion that most communities of faith function simply as "self-serving clubs."

CONCLUSION

We have seen that congregations have much to offer to their communities. They are stable institutions that train and deploy many volunteers. They provide actual economic benefits to their local neighborhoods and regions. These capacities for social activism become more and more relevant as religious leaders and congregations display a renewed interest in cities.

Numerous studies clearly show that the world continues to become more urbanized. In 1900, about 14 percent of the world's population lived in cities. By 2050, we expect the number will be closer to 70 percent. Churches have taken notice. Perhaps there is no better example than white evangelicals, a religious group that has been almost synonymous with suburbanization in the United States. Scholars have been tracking a renewed interest in the city on the part of white evangelicals. Some of this interest shows up in parachurch movements like the Christian Community Development Association and in congregational associations like the Community of Communities and the Acts 29 Network. But we are also seeing that mostly white suburban evangelical megachurches have started to focus congregational mission efforts on core city projects. In some instances, these have been interpreted as ways for the congregations to gain legitimacy, reflecting the strong awareness and feeling that churches need to have some form of social service or community engagement to be seen as doing the proper work of the church.

Additionally, some churches have explicitly chosen to stay in urban contexts and frequently see that decision as a significant aspect of their history and crucial to their identity. So, while past studies described an "uneasiness" in the relationship between churches and cities, more recent developments indicate that many congregations embrace their urban identity. They are comfortable in their urban location. Such a trend merits close scrutiny.

Recent studies also indicate that some central city populations have been growing faster than those of outlying suburbs for the first time since the 1920s. Moreover, some scholars have asserted that some religious traditions (including white evangelicals) are "re-urbanizing." Because of theological convictions, they feel called to live in urban contexts. As churches reach out to the cities or remain in urban places, they can have a vibrant influence. And they see local engagement as closely linked to how they identify as a faith community. But as we will see in the next chapter, churches must also reckon with their history, challenges, and limitations.

Challenges
in the Churches

4

INSIDERS AND OUTSIDERS

Emmanuel Church is located in a core city neighborhood in a Great Lakes city. It is an historically white ethnic congregation. But it has struggled to maintain its membership rolls as the neighborhood has changed from mostly white to mostly African American. Over the last four decades, the membership of the church has dropped from a peak of 800 to about 150 today. A colleague and I used mapping software and church directory addresses to take snapshots of the average distance of a member's residence from the church over the course of those forty years. We learned that in 1970 members tended to live about two miles from church. By 2010, the distance increased to about five miles. In other words, as the neighborhood changed from almost 70 percent white to 35 percent white, the members of the church decided to live farther and farther away. Indeed, when I presented my research at the church, one member told me, "We aren't a church *of* the community; we are a church *for* the community." The congregation clearly assumed that they would be unable to attract members from within the church neighborhood.

Despite the good work of congregations outlined in chapter 3, churches like Emmanuel may have a complicated history with their neighborhoods. Sure, they offer an intimate community that makes people feel less anonymous and alienated from city life. But these internal relationships may come at the expense of developing external relationships. Churches seem to be better at helping people in the church know one another than in helping the church become part of the broader community. In the words of political scientists, congregations have been better at nurturing "bonding ties" (between insiders) than "bridging ties" (linking insiders to outsiders).

A study of congregations in a district of Boston revealed these limitations. The churches there found it fairly easy to nurture internal networks. They eagerly responded to the needs that existed *within* their church-based social networks. If someone from within the congregation needed help and came to a church, they quickly offered assistance. But the energy of the Boston churches was unfocused, and it did not center on their own neighborhoods. Since members tended to live in scattered patterns throughout the city, they did not really "see" the "outside" neighborhood right around the church. Some churches even tended to "disregard neighborhoods as sources of membership and objects of mission."

Most of the churches in this district functioned as internal communities that *just happened* to be located within the geographic bounds of particular neighborhoods. They did not develop neighborhood relationships. They did not act as the "node" of a neighborhood. Consequently, they did not foster neighborhood cohesion. They were not social spaces where neighborhood relationships could be enhanced. They did not provide a hub for social services that would bond the church to the neighborhood. The author of this study argued that these churches primarily invested in activities that "served the survival and growth strategies of the congregations themselves" rather than benefitting the local community. As a result, these churches seemed irrelevant to their own neighborhoods. Even worse, for six days a week, they acted as dead spots within the neighborhood.

Of course, sometimes churches consciously do not engage with their neighborhoods because they are trying to fill a particular niche. In other words, they are trying to appeal to a certain type of person. It's why some megachurches offer multiple worship styles in varying venues—everything from a coffee shop to heavy metal to skateboarding themes. Congregational studies, though, tell us that churches used to be more place-based. They drew attenders from the surrounding neighborhood, no matter how different those people might be from one another. However, in recent decades, churches have become more niche-oriented. They draw attenders from throughout a metropolitan area, and attenders are attracted to the particular identity that the church projects. These "boutique" churches have less at stake in their particular locations. They think less about engaging the neighborhood and more about what kind of worship or programming will attract attenders. What will cause someone to drive by other churches to attend this congregation on a weekly basis?

Growing churches also tend to be homogeneous. In fact, research has shown that churches in the United States have become intense sites of clusters. "Clusters" is a term that social scientists give to groups composed of members who are very much alike. In general, the population of the United States is sorting into ever more extreme affinity groups (where everyone shares the same identities and interests) or clusters. Congregations have not been immune to this trend. Overall, churches in the United States are *more segregated* than neighborhoods.

In some cases, the principle of "like attracts like" has been an intentional church growth strategy. However, even when churches do not intentionally try to cluster, they find that their attenders look similar, make comparable amounts of money, possess similar educations, and even tend to vote the same way. Some of this clustering has to do with people simply wanting to be comfortable and affirmed. Such homogeneity, though, tends to isolate people in ways that prevent them from fully understanding the problems and perspectives of people who are different from them. When churches are defined by the particular kinds of people who attend, they can lose sight of a missional commitment to their own neighborhood.

What the focus on "insiders" and nurturing "bonding ties" tells us is that churches who want to be good neighbors will need to be *intentional* about becoming good neighbors It is not easy to nurture "bridging ties." It is easier to cluster into an affinity group.

MAINTAINING CONGREGATIONAL HEALTH

Another challenge that churches face is changing neighborhoods. Scholars who study congregations have found the metaphor of ecology useful as they consider how congregations adapt, or don't adapt, to their contexts. In other words, we can think of congregations as organisms that need nutrients to survive and thrive. Traditionally, churches reflected the population that lived in the surrounding neighborhood. As long as the people who lived there had some kind of theological or ethnic connection to the church, it likely would survive. However, city neighborhoods tend to be fairly fluid environments. Groups of people may change quite quickly. A neighborhood that once was predominantly Jewish may become Irish, then African American, then Laotian. Thus, the churches in that neighborhood will experience an unstable ecology where the nutrients keep changing.

In a changing neighborhood, urban churches have three choices. They may adapt and change their practices in order to attract the incoming population. Or they may highlight an aspect of their identity so that people will be willing to drive distances, past other congregations, to attend their particular church. Or they can simply follow their familiar population to a new environment. If we use the ecology metaphor, we could say that the congrega-tion needs to draw on its nutrient-rich environment. Or it needs to reach into the corners of the metro region to pull in nutrients (attenders). Or it needs to uproot itself and move to a new nutrient-rich home. The metaphor of ecology illustrates how congregations act like organisms bent on survival. That is, the natural instinct of churches is to selfishly maintain their own health.

Again, if a city church wants to become a good neighbor, it must face up to the challenge of adapting and changing its practices in order to fit into a changing environment.

CONFLICTING UNDERSTANDINGS OF POVERTY

Churches who want to serve their neighborhoods face another challenge. Many church members have conflict-ing explanations about how socioeconomic systems have marginalized millions of people in the United States. A recent study reported that certain Christians in America are twice as likely as the general population to blame a person's poverty on a lack of effort. Congregational lead-ers and members often think this way about poor people in their neighborhoods, and most evangelical Christians believe in the "miracle motif." This is the idea that if people would just convert to Christianity and take more personal responsibility, their finances would automatically become less of a problem. Many Christians in the United States have also generally emphasized a personal relationship with God and conversion narratives. These two emphases tend to bias them toward assuming that individuals are primarily responsible for being poor. Such an attitude assumes that a person's poverty has mostly to do with personal moral failings.

Social scientific evidence, however, points to systems that have failed poor people. These systems include access to education, health care, job training, real estate loans, and transportation. When parents lack ready access to these essential social benefits, their children's lives are also compromised. Poverty is perpetuated across generations. And the social science evidence clearly shows that these systems are more significant in causing poverty than lack of effort or faulty values.

These conflicting notions of how we explain persistent poverty came to me forcefully during a meeting of deacons at my church. I attend a largely white congregation situated in a core city neighborhood. The neighborhood bears all the hallmarks of urban distress. For decades, there were few jobs, few economic or social investments in the neighborhood, and rampant racial segregation. Now, long-time residents worry that the forces of gentrification will push them out of their homes as rising rents have de-stabilized the housing market. Deacons, rightfully so, focus much of their time on being good stewards of the congregation's finances. So whenever we started discussing neighborhood needs, we found ourselves in difficult conversations about who does and does not *deserve* funds from the church. A typical conversation sounded like this:

Deacon 1: We have another request from Mary. This time for a water bill. She owes well over $1,000, and the city will turn her water off next week if the bill is not paid.

Deacon 2: And that would be terrible—she has young children living in her house!

Deacon 3: But it seems like we get a benevolence request from her every other month, and when we give her money, it doesn't seem to make much of a difference. Is this a good use of congregational funds?

Deacon 2: Well, it's kind of the nature of underemployment—really difficult to get out from under bills that have been piling up.

Deacon 3: Yeah, right, I get that, but I wonder if we could help her with financial management. You know, walk alongside her as she makes decisions about her money and where it should go. Accountability.

Deacon 1: Right. That's a good idea. We're supposed to be stewards of the church's money—it really makes sense to develop relationships with the people who receive the funds . . . to make sure they aren't wasting it.

Deacon 3: Perhaps we could even help Mary set up a budget?

Deacon 2: Sure. We could. But what good is a budget when you have job that simply doesn't pay enough to meet expenses? And is that our role as deacons? After all, we're not a social service agency.

Deacon: 1: Yes, but what good is it to give money if there isn't some kind of lifestyle change?

[uncomfortable silence]

Most of our monthly meetings, and all the email conversations between meetings, were taken up with making decisions about similar requests. It could be that we had forgotten that, in the early church, charity rested on the assumption that as Christians give to those requesting aid, they give to Christ himself. In addition, a primary difficulty is that we understood the *sources* of poverty in different ways. Is the primary cause of poverty the moral decisions individuals make? Or is poverty caused by a system in which individuals are trapped and in which there simply are not equal opportunities for everyone? We had to wrestle with this question. How do people find themselves in situations so desperate that they need to formally request a church to help them pay their light, water, or gas bill?

My own research has revealed that many Christians in the United States continue to be convinced that the poor suffer from a "culture of poverty." In other words, they tend to see the poor as being caught in lifestyles that are outside of the middle class or the mainstream. Those lifestyles are passed down through generations and continue to perpetuate poverty. Individual choices are then blamed for an individual's or a family's poverty. So if it's about choices, then changes in lifestyle will be the ultimate remedy.

In interviews, I have repeatedly been struck by the way churchgoers from various religious traditions assume that issues of poverty are best addressed through personal relationships or through a conversion experience. That is, they believe that helping people out of poverty requires that church members show them how they might *choose* to live differently. They rarely recognize the institutional problems that haunt millions of the poor in the United States. They do not understand that these problems inhibit or even prohibit the poor from moving out of poverty.

For example, numerous studies show that where and to whom you are born are the two most significant predictors of social and economic attainment in the United States. In other words, things that are outside of an individual's control drive life chances more than any cultural values or behavioral patterns. These include where you go to school, the safety of your neighborhood, how much income your family earns, how much wealth your parents can generate, access to quality healthcare, access to nutritious food, the types of available transportation, and so forth. To be sure, lifestyle choices can have an influence, but they are less important to the perpetuation of poverty than larger systems.

Social science studies show us that poverty is *not* best understood as being produced by cultural shortcomings. There are simply not the same opportunities and resources for everyone. It is a system failure rather than a personal failure. But it gets worse. For instance, researchers have found hidden costs to being poor that many middle-class families do not experience.

An example of those hidden costs includes the inability to have easy access to bargains at stores like Costco or Sam's Club. First, those stores tend to assume an individual automobile ownership that simply does not exist among many poor families. The stores tend to be located in unwalkable areas and are frequently not situated near good public transportation options. Second, the nature of "bulk-buying" assumes that a one-time high cost buy of toilet paper or cereal will pay off in the long run because the price per unit is cheaper when purchased in larger quantities. Such a transaction, though, demands a measure of disposable income that impoverished families and individuals, by definition, do not have. In other words, poor families cannot even *save* money in the same manner as many more affluent families. In fact, it takes money to save money.

As churches seek to be good neighbors in poor communities, they must realize that poverty is not a simple or individual social "ailment." It cannot be cured merely through personal relationships or lifestyle choices. Congregations will need to understand the power of institutions and social systems. They will need to reconsider how they have typically engaged the poor in their own neighborhoods.

FINDING A NEIGHBORHOOD TO ENGAGE

In the past, as we saw with Emmanuel Church, church members tended to be neighborhood residents. Because they lived in the neighborhood, these members engaged in community activities. They were simply part of the community. It was the place that felt secure, familiar, and comfortable. This scenario is still true of some churches.

However, recent research on city churches shows a different picture. Often, if a congregation recognizes that they have many resources while their local neighborhood has few, they will become actively involved with the community. They will seek to meet the needs of their local neighborhood. On the other hand, if the community resources and the church resources appear to be similarly abundant, the congregation may look for other neighborhoods to serve. In other words, when congregational members and neighborhood residents are different from one another, churches may become more deeply engaged in social services in their local communities. But when congregational members and neighborhood residents are similarly affluent, churches may look farther afield for communities in which to become engaged.

This development may not be altogether a good thing. In fact, the advent of more engaged, missional churches has led to a tendency to seek out sites of "otherness." For example, suburban megachurches with largely white membership tend to target neighborhoods in the core city for social service. One recent study found that two largely white suburban Knoxville megachurches displayed a "particular fascination with the city." The author warned, however, that for these churches, the core city of Knoxville represented a "localized otherness and disorder." In fact, the largely white churches showed much more interest in outreach to African Americans in Knoxville than they did to poor whites in the nearby Appalachian Mountains, which emphasized their perception of a moral and social breakdown in the core city. Church members saw themselves as both qualified and obliged to help fix these core urban neighborhoods. In addition, the targeted core city neighborhoods were not close by. This distance allowed congregational members to visit only when it was convenient for them. These paternalistic attitudes caused problems both for churches and for neighborhoods and point out the need for congregations to learn how best to engage their *local* communities.

CONCLUSION

Churches have limitations. They are better at nurturing "binding ties" than "bridging ties." They may find it difficult to adapt to a changing neighborhood. They may resist understanding the systemic nature of deep poverty. They often find it easier to help the more distant "other" than to engage their own neighborhoods. And one of their great strengths—hundreds of trained volunteers—also speaks to the relative scarcity of professionals on staff in their congregations. Given these limitations, congregations probably should not see themselves as alternatives to government social service programs.

Moreover, we should be wary of overemphasizing the role of social engagement and service within congregations. Most congregations highly value social service. But it remains one of many activities on which they expend energy and resources. Congregations, then, should not be seen as magic bullets for all of society's ills. They are not a substitute for public sector programs and support. In other words, congregations serve best when they complement existing social services—not when they seek to replace those programs. Congregations should be ready to accept their limitations as social service providers. Though they have resources and capacities, they simply do not have the infrastructure and expertise to run social service agencies. Such a careful distinction should remain in the consciousness of all churches focused on community engagement.

What Churches Offer

5

CHURCHES IN CHANGING NEIGHBORHOODS

If churches should not replace public social service agencies, what should they do? As we saw in chapter 4, neighborhoods change, districts change, and cities change. Racial and class demographics shift. Churches are affected by these changes. For instance, many members may move out of the local neighborhood. But churches can also influence and affect changes themselves—whether they realize it or not. As changes sweep over their neighborhoods, how should congregations respond?

Many city churches feel hamstrung by the fact that few, if any, of their members actually live in their neighborhood. They have lost the intimate ties they once had to the neighborhood. Some churches rightly worry that they may blunder into doing things that the neighborhood residents find useless or, in some cases, actually harmful. The question then becomes how to avoid counter-productive activities in the community.

What we know, however, is that even a congregation that is not very active is still a presence in the urban landscape. A church's influence is never non-existent. Congregations don't always fully grasp the significance they might have in their neighborhood. For instance, one study found that seemingly vulnerable storefront churches often contribute to neighborhood vitality in surprising ways. Their mere presence helps to stabilize neighborhood real estate values—more so than even freestanding churches. So it is important that congregations make an effort to learn how to become good neighbors.

SEEING THINGS WITH "FRESH EYES"

One tool churches can employ is to look at themselves and their familiar neighborhood with "fresh eyes." They should identify patterns and habits that have become so normal that insiders within the congregation have difficulty recognizing them. Fresh eyes can help congregations see the valuable resources and assets that they actually have at their disposal. For instance, one Canadian study identified five things that congregations may be able to contribute to the broader community: 1) open space; 2) education; 3) individual programs; 4) community development; and 5) community trust and care.

Open space includes many areas a church might take for granted. Seldom used parking lots or side lawns may become community garden plots. Recreational play structures for children and athletic fields for all ages can be opened to the neighborhood. The church may allow free parking throughout the week in their parking lot. Education includes nursery school and day care, after school programs, mentoring, and tutoring. Individual programs include suicide prevention, hosting Alcoholics Anonymous meetings, identifying employment opportunities, crime prevention, community and parish nursing, refugee re-settlement, and promoting youth civic engagement—to name but a few. Community development includes job training and housing initiatives. Community trust and care includes providing volunteer hours inside a safe building. All these "goods" might be so familiar to church leaders and members that they fail to recognize them for what they are.

USING BUILDINGS

Another way to think about community engagement is to take an inventory of how resources in the church may be used. The building that a congregation worships in is likely one of its primary assets. Indeed, the church building is typically one of the most visible and accessible places in a community, and these features alone have value. The physical places can enable and enrich a congregation's life. The building also tends to help define a congregation's identity. Rightly or wrongly, assumptions are made about the church with the tall brick steeple and the complex stain glass windows on the most prominent corner of the city. Different assumptions are made about the congregation meeting in the ramshackle bowling alley with the weed-infested gravel parking lot located on the outskirts.

Church buildings can be used in many ways if both members and neighbors think carefully and creatively about them. First, however, congregations must understand what they have. They should look with fresh eyes at their own buildings. Second, they should consider a number of paths forward to use the buildings more effectively. Third, they should take steps to be attentive and responsive to the neighborhood's welfare. Fourth, any decisions about building changes should include both members and neighbors.

Congregational experts suggest conducting surveys that enable local residents to offer their advice or holding a day-long community forum where neighbors, businesses, social service agencies, and civic leaders offer ideas. In the latter case, churches might even become aware of potential new partnership opportunities. A thorough understanding of the building allows congregations to respond to their own identity and mission as well as to the needs of the neighborhood. When the congregation and the broader community collaborate and communicate well, good and lasting alliances develop.

USING COMMITMENT

In addition to building resources, congregations also have the commitment of members. This is no small thing. The erosion of community ties and trust in the last few decades in the United States has been duly noted. In fact, social scientists have remarked that Americans have so retreated into private life that public pastimes like bowling leagues are becoming scarce.

Yet many churches have largely withstood these changes and many remain vibrant centers of human activity and attachment. Congregations sometimes take these bonded relationships and commitments for granted. They are too familiar and obvious to recognize. But congregations can mobilize their members and remind them of their moral responsibility to initiate action. And they can offer reinforcement and support by surrounding members with people who care about the same issues.

As churches mobilize their members, congregational leaders should ask two important questions. First, how familiar are the community needs to members of the congregation? Second, does the church have identifiable special-interest groups who are interested in specific types of services or programming? By way of example, think about this. Have you ever wondered why so many congregations have food pantries while so few have ministries to people with AIDS? The reason has much to do with familiarity. Congregations have a long history of food support, and it is a well-publicized need. On the other hand, AIDS support ministries have a much shorter history and are less familiar for many churches.

In order to enhance their ministries, congregations might engage in ethnography. That is, they should study the culture of their neighborhood and their church by participating in community events and interviewing neighbors. This approach requires time and energy and analyzing the congregation and their neighbors in a careful, disciplined way. But this effort will allow congregations to hear different voices as members engage the community and listen to interviews.

USING EDUCATION

Congregations also typically offer some type of religious education. It might seem obvious, but in order to sustain the organization, they must find ways to recruit and socialize new members. Moreover, even longtime attenders need to be reminded what the church believes and how they understand their identity compared to other congregations. Because of this, churches must become expert at instruction and teaching. Education remains crucial for the continued success of the church. Almost every religious tradition asks believers to be ethical, not to cheat, not to cause harm, and to be charitable and generous in their behavior. Churches could think more carefully about how they have fostered a culture of learning within the church. How might that experience be extended to the broader community?

USING PROCESSES

In some ways, churches are similar to other nonprofit organizations: they plan, they pay bills, they write reports, they hold meetings, and they maintain property. All of these processes require skills. These skills, in turn, might be used not just in the church but in the community as well. In fact, members tend to assume that their church will provide some kind of social service, and they expect to be asked to contribute. For example, some congregations have begun lending programs while others have acted as incubators for small business and non-profits.

USING VOLUNTEERS

Almost all volunteers in the United States donate some of their time to a congregation. Moreover, one quarter of *all* volunteering occurs within a church. Most churches also have paid staff who dedicate at least a few hours every week to overseeing some type of social engagement. And as we have seen, most congregations have building space where they host service or community-oriented events. In short, congregations tend to have rich resources and capacities for volunteering in the community.

Moreover, people who show up regularly for worship also tend to do more volunteer work in their communities. Social scientists recognize that churches are "sites of social capital production." That means churches are places where people work together to make one another's lives better. The "capital" they produce is not mere money. It is social interaction and familiarity. It is "capital" because in times of trouble, people can draw on this goodwill and work together. Sociologist Nancy Ammerman has argued that anyone interested in seeing instances of social capital being developed should spend some time in churches. It is within congregations, according to Ammerman, that community ties are strengthened and both social and material resources are shared. Other social scientists argue that congregations provide the "glue" that binds a society together.

CONCLUSION

Congregations have many resources. Frequently, though, these remain so familiar and taken for granted that leaders and members don't see them for what they are. These resources may be "hard and countable" or "soft and relational." Hard resources include "money, people, staff, and buildings." Soft resources include "shared experiences of coming through difficult times, connections to other institutions, and the strength of members' commitment to the congregation." These soft resources may be difficult to fully appreciate, but they have a very real value.

Despite anxiety over the rise of the "nones," those individuals like Will in chapter 2 who claim to have no religious affiliation, studies clearly indicate that congregations remain significant institutions in the United States. In fact, more Americans affiliate with religious congregations than with any other type of association, group, or club. The sheer numbers of membership and levels of their commitment make churches potential influential hubs of their communities.

What congregations need to do is to assess carefully, with fresh eyes, their own resources and assets. Then, in conversation with residents in their neighborhood, they can begin to map out ways in which these resources can be used to benefit the entire community.

Relationships
and Systems

6

ADDRESSING SYSTEMIC INJUSTICE

James Robertson, a fifty-six-year-old Detroiter, commutes twenty-three miles each way to work five days a week. Ordinarily, we might expect a journey of that distance to take half an hour—or maybe an hour if traffic is bad. However, since Robertson's 1988 Honda Accord broke down, he's found himself relying on a haphazard public transportation system and his own two legs. His daily commute now includes twenty-one miles of walking. At $10.55 an hour, Robertson can't afford to buy, maintain, and insure a car in Detroit. Robertson's employer, Schain Mold & Injection, is located in the suburb of Rochester Hills—a no-bus land. Rochester Hills is one of forty Detroit area municipalities where voters opted out of paying a transit millage. Robertson's daily routine has him leaving the house at 8:00 am and returning at 4:00 am. Despite all this, he has a perfect attendance record at work. Robertson is an example of a core city resident who has been failed by a system. Yet, he perseveres.

The systemic injustice faced by James Robertson remains largely hidden and difficult for many churches to see. Congregations have resources. But how should they be used not just to help James Robertson, but also to address the problem of shoddy public transportation systems that disproportionately affect people who can't afford cars?

As we saw in chapter 4, churches tend naturally to create relationships as ways to engage their neighborhoods and address issues of poverty. This is all well and good. However, it may not be enough. There are also profound examples of congregations acting in effective ways to influence public systems and policies.

For instance, the Sisters of St. Casimir, who run Holy Cross Hospital and Maria High School in Chicago, saw that predatory lending practices had decimated their church's neighborhood. One sister said, "We've lived in this neighborhood a long time [since 1911], and we've seen the abandoned houses, just like everyone else. Our community has never been involved in politics or issues like this. We were focused on religion and our own institutions." The sisters, though, decided that they could not simply stand by and "let the market prevail" in regard to housing losses and blight. To do so, they concluded, would be to allow the neighborhood to be destroyed. So they began to actively participate in protests against the lending practices while also starting a strategic program to educate neighbors about how to avoid being sold a predatory loan.

Another example is storefront churches in core city neighborhoods that have been abandoned by the white middle class residents, factories, and retail stores. One researcher reported,

> Some inner-city churches are large, established congregations that can draw people from the

suburbs to help with their programs, but store-front churches are a better example of the struggles of inner-city residents as they try to engage community reform. Many such churches are small enough to give members a strong sense of belonging, compared with larger or less democratically organized groups. They provide opportunities to learn civic skills, such as how to speak in public, how to knock on doors, or how to keep a budget or put together a newsletter.

In this way, storefront churches, often dismissed as insignificant, actually act as primary players in combatting neighborhood problems. Research has found that residents who were not attenders of churches still noticed the work that congregations in their neighborhood did to address problems in their community. With that in mind, it becomes more pressing for churches to consider how they might influence systems and structures. Relationship building is not enough.

A REBIRTH OF CITIES

To begin, churches need to understand the role of cities. There is a renewed interest in urban places. Cities seem recently to have captured the popular imagination in the United States. Research indicates that some core cities have begun to "thrive at the expense of suburbs." Stories in *The*

New York Times herald the recovery of America's most broken major city, Detroit, by noting the influx of tech firms, coffee shops, entertainment districts, and urban farmers.

However, cities remain complex—and sometimes contradictory—places. Even while we seem to be in the midst of an urban renaissance, there is no shaking free from the fact that many urban neighborhoods remain mired and forgotten in their decades-old poverty. These are not the places where you find a food truck or that you see lampooned on an episode of the IFC television show "Portlandia." The "Creative Class"—artists, food truck chefs, baristas, tech start-ups—tends not to move here. And without proper access to grocery stores or even small markets, these neighborhoods will struggle to ever become "walkable." An immovable type of poverty seems to have etched itself into the streets, sidewalks, and homes of these neighborhoods. Perhaps most worrying, research has shown that children who find themselves raised in these places have limited hope for achieving social and economic mobility.

Similarly, some poorer racial minorities have been pushed into older, inner ring suburbs. As elites move back into city centers, gentrification occurs. Previously beleaguered urban neighborhoods see significant investment in housing, amenities, and new businesses as families with high socio-economic status see it as a desirable residential location. As rents and taxes rise with revitalization, longtime residents are forced to relocate to other neighborhoods.

Although gentrification should not be overlooked or dismissed, some scholars argue that concentrated urban poverty remains a more pressing socio-economic issue. For instance if we take a four-decade look at impoverished neighborhoods, we see that only a small percentage have experienced a shift in poverty rates that fall below the national average. In other words, there are few instances of poor neighborhoods that have been transformed into more stable socio-economic communities. In fact, the trends since 1970 show the particularly distressing stranglehold poverty has maintained—and even strengthened—on some urban neighborhoods.

High poverty neighborhoods are defined as places where 30 percent or more of the population live below the poverty line. From 1970 to 2010, the number of poor people in the United States living in these high poverty neighborhoods more than doubled from two million to four million. Moreover, the number of high poverty neighborhoods nearly tripled from 1,100 to 3,100. At the same time, only about 100 of those 1,100 high poverty neighborhoods in 1970 saw significant declines in poverty in the following decades. In sum, the last forty years have seen only a few occurrences of gentrification and reductions in poverty. During that same stretch of decades, the number of high poverty neighborhoods increased.

What do these statistics mean for churches? At the very least, they mean that congregations should not turn their backs on city neighborhoods. Instead, they should try to mobilize their resources in creative and cooperative ways to help solve deep-seated issues of neighborhood poverty. The complexities of poverty and neighborhood renewal will not be solved merely through relationships and conversions, as the following two case studies reveal.

CASE STUDIES FROM CONNECTICUT AND MICHIGAN

A 1984 study of Hartford, Connecticut attempted to track how congregations engaged their communities. The authors outlined four different types of religious presence. One type of church they labeled "evangelistic." As might be expected, these churches promoted activities that had the goal of conversion, getting people to become Christians and come to church regularly. A second type they described as "activist." These churches wanted to change the world in ways that they interpreted to be more just. A third category of churches the authors labeled "civic." These congregations understood themselves to be pillars of the community and sought to be anchoring social institutions that people could look to for leadership. A fourth and final type of church the authors identified as "sanctuary." These congregations tended to be highly internal and focused on heavenly issues as opposed to earthly.

In 2014, colleagues and I conducted a similar study in Grand Rapids, Michigan, and interviewed congregants about their churches' community engagement practices.

We found that rather than falling into specific types, most congregations took multiple approaches to neighborhood involvement. Most of the churches emphasized building relationships. Fewer engaged with social systems. However, some interviewees discussed multiple programs that sought to build relationships, but also acknowledged the significance of systems. An attender of an urban Catholic church, responding to a question about the congregation's involvement in the neighborhood, related the following wide range of activities:

> It is an ongoing discussion of what is helping. Just this morning, I got a voicemail from the father on working with Goodwill, who is now renting our old school building, to work with them to provide a weekly luncheon. But we want it to be more than just food. We want ACCESS [All County Congregations Emergency Support Service] to be involved; we would like the nurses to be involved. To provide more than just food, but to address more needs that anybody coming in might need. Once a year we do a health fair for seniors where we give them flu shots and provide resources on issues they might have questions about. When those Medicare plans were being thrown around, we had info on the plans, and government representatives came in and explained things. We have a fish fry every Lent. It's a huge draw because it's

very inexpensive, and it's all you can eat fish. But we do it more as a community service than for profit.

This urban Catholic church offered opportunities for both relationship building and for thinking about the systems that affected local residents.

In another case, when asked to describe his church's relationship to the neighborhood, a man attending a suburban Catholic congregation responded:

You know, I think we used to talk a lot about that. . . [and] I know there's always been a strong commitment. We actually gave one of our church buildings to house a neighborhood association and low-income senior apartments. So, there's been a real physical commitment. There's a health clinic in the basement of the church. . . . You know that kind of thing really supports the neighborhood.

Some members of other congregations spoke of meeting physical needs but also recognized that social systems needed to be addressed. But these members rarely acknowledged that their respective congregations were doing anything atypical or unexpected. Most, in fact, tended to speak rather matter-of-factly. The following from an attender of a mainline Protestant church is typical:

This church does a variety of random outreach things.... There's a daycare and a refugee resettling program, things like that. In terms of the neighborhood, it's just sort of "the church that's there"; maybe it adds to property values or something. There's a lot of ministry within the congregation, but a lot of the outreach takes the form of ministry within the church hierarchy. Bishops get together and decide that "we're going to do this," and then that's what happens.

Health care clinics, neighborhood associations, refugee resettlement, and low-income daycare are programs that may nurture relationships. But they are also programs that address systemic issues. They take into account that many in the community face structural barriers that limit their opportunities to live better lives.

CONCLUSION

Churches tend to be places full of relationships. Thus, it should probably not be surprising that many congregations find themselves attracted to the idea of relationship-building as a method of social engagement. However, as churches turn fresh eyes on their resources and on their neighborhood, they should begin to identify ways to build up the neighborhood around them. To really address issues of poverty, merely developing relationships is inadequate. A friendly relationship has no effect on health care coverage. Individual conversions do not necessarily change systems of injustice. As churches continue to be good neighbors in their communities, they can develop ways to broaden their concern with individuals to include addressing the systemic barriers to well-being that those individuals face.

Working Together

7

BARRIERS TO CONGREGATIONAL COLLABORATION

I recently conducted interviews with pastors who were pursuing a certificate program at a local seminary. The pastors were thankful for this educational opportunity, which was fully funded by the generosity of a local foundation. But some said they had reservations about one aspect of the program: occasional pulpit trades. One pastor confided his concerns, "I don't want anyone to steal my sheep." Others indicated they felt too overwhelmed maintaining their own congregation to enjoy the luxury of visiting another worship service. It seemed to me that fear and busyness kept these pastors from pursuing collaborative projects.

What is true for pastors is true for their churches. Despite the strong evidence that congregations tend to be active in their communities, we also know that they rarely cooperate or network with other congregations. They have trouble finding ways to work together, even when they reside in the same neighborhood or the same block. This resistance to cooperation is probably due to "de facto congregationalism." That is, churches in the United States tend to act independently, even when they are members of a denomination or association. Just as individuals value freedom and autonomy within the political structure, churches prefer to pursue a local agenda that they see as fitting their own community. Because churches like to act alone, they tend to run programs that do the same things. These "silo programs" are redundant, inefficient, and sometimes even competitive. Because they act independently, churches frequently fail to see opportunities to cooperate that might actually help their communities.

It is not that churches dislike one another. Or that they are uninterested in cooperating. Rather, the Kent County study referenced earlier revealed that fully 92 percent of religious leaders in the county expressed an interest in working with other congregations on "broad-based efforts to improve community well-being." In addition, research from other scholars reveals that congregations possess a unique ability to mobilize thousands of members across a geographic region. Congregations working together have the social and moral standing to push attenders to consider not just their own self-interests, but also their care for fellow human beings. Churches can make a strong case that their members should be interested in serving the community together because of their common commitment to a belief system.

SORTING AND CLUSTERING

There is another barrier to working together, namely the subtext in many urban neighborhoods of race. Recent research regarding churches and race is fairly depressing.

First, of course, we should address the cliché that "the most segregated hour of Christian America is eleven o›clock on Sunday morning." That claim, indeed, seems to have staying power. In fact, it turns out that as people in the United States sort and cluster into ever more extreme affinity groups, churches have not been immune. In his 2008 book *The Big Sort*, author Bill Bishop clearly shows that churches in this country are more segregated than neighborhoods. And to be clear, neighborhoods remain extremely segregated.

The goal for churches in the past was to *transform* the "social tenets of those who came through the door." In direct contrast, "now people go to a church not for how it might change their beliefs, but for how their precepts will be reconfirmed." Indeed, University of Maryland political scientist James Gimpel finds "very little evidence that churches are really transforming their congregations. . . . It is rather quite the reverse. Ministers depend on pleasing a particular congregation for their longevity." In other words, ministers remain wary of actually offending congregants. Gimpel continues, "It's conformity all the way."

Bishop also describes a similar situation: "We have more choices than ever before in the hundreds of religious niche markets. But given a choice, we select sameness." Ordinary church members agree. One attender told some sociologists that "I think the whole concept of blacks and whites worshipping together is great, but how can you do that when you feel so uncomfortable?" Indeed, my own ethnographic research has indicated that churches tend to use the worship service to reinforce a sense of belonging. That is, worship makes the insiders feel more like insiders. It affirms their beliefs and lifestyles. Challenges by congregational leaders to beliefs and lifestyles are dangerous because in the church marketplace, there are plenty of other options for worshippers.

COMPETITIVE MARKETS

It may sound strange, but congregations often act as competitors. For example, congregational leaders realize that if they fail to offer something the attenders want, then the attenders just might choose a worship location down the street or across the city that offers more of what they desire. Sometimes congregations are very conscious of what they offer and whom they want to attract. Sometimes they make these choices more subconsciously. When it comes to offering services to the neighborhood, churches may also be in competition with one another. If a congregation does nothing to help those in need while its neighbor is known as a benevolent church that goes above and beyond for the larger community, the first church may suffer.

At times, however, there is no collaboration and no competition. There are simply many churches in one neighborhood who each act independently. One study of Chicago's neighborhoods reported that there might actually be a negative relationship between a high density of churches and neighborhood well-being and levels of trust. If many of the congregants come from *outside* the community and do not directly engage with the community, it may appear that the neighborhood is being invaded by non-residents every Sunday morning. The resulting dynamic is a mismatch which "is especially common in low-income black areas that continue to draw middle-class parishioners that have migrated to other residential neighborhoods in the suburbs or far reaches of the city." The article's author concludes that "trust in one's fellow man is apparently not enhanced by the church."

BENEFITS OF CONGREGATIONAL COLLABORATION

Scholars who study congregations note that if churches want to do more for their communities, they will have to learn how to cooperate with each other. Small, independent congregations frequently feel vulnerable. They have fluctuating budgets and finances on which they cannot depend. Because of these liabilities, they assume they are unable to sustain anything more than token efforts at wider community engagement. Some lack of networks, of course, is due to the decline of denominations. Where congregations might traditionally have allied themselves with neighboring churches of the same denomination, these opportunities are currently less available. Denominational resources and loyalty have declined. It also seems that larger congregations sometimes prefer to keep control over their resources rather than networking or collaborating with other churches.

But forming coalitions and alliances among congregations enhances the effectiveness of social engagement. First, the networks offer a higher profile and clear indications that the participating congregations care enough about the well-being of the greater community to work together for its benefit. Second, congregations may have niches or skills at which they are more adept than others. For example, one church may have a cohort of computer engineers who are technologically savvy. Another may boast a well-organized crew of kitchen volunteers who know how to both cook tasty food and manage its distribution. Similarly, the churches may have buildings that complement one another. For instance, one church may have a good-sized industrial kitchen while another has a playground with new equipment and open space. Neighboring churches could take inventories of their assets and pool their resources.

As they conduct these inventories, congregations might see themselves as part of a community ecology. They belong to a habitat where they interact with other organisms, such as nonprofits, schools, businesses, government, people, and other churches. Each entity has its own place in the habitat. It both influences and is influenced by the presence and activities of the other organisms. Congregations who understand their surroundings (or ecology) are in the best position to offer programming that actually serves the community.

There are instances of congregations that have come together with others to address a common social issue. In Grand Rapids, Michigan, a diverse group of churches, with the support of a local foundation, developed a program to address academic underachievement in the city. The foundation recruited forty churches to help design and implement a pilot program. First, the church representatives identified the problems and brainstormed about ways the churches might best use their resources to improve educational outcomes in Grand Rapids. Then in the following weeks, the representatives designed, modified, and refined plans for a new program. They wanted churches to harness their best assets to promote education in the city.

The program they developed was called the Family Leadership Initiative (FLI). The pilot program centered on two-and-a-half-hour weekly meetings scheduled during the academic semester. The template for the meetings included one hour of family bonding that focused on the value of communication. In the second hour, children could receive academic mentoring and homework help. During the same hour, the parents gathered for parent training classes and discussion. The evening closed with thirty minutes of worship that included reflections about the preceding two hours, prayer, and singing. The children provided some leadership during the closing worship.

By the end of the pilot program, 290 families (1,084 individuals) had participated. Participants reported a high level of appreciation. Eighty-five percent of participants agreed that they were satisfied with their family's experience in the program. Moreover, 96 percent of parents rated the overall quality of the program as good, very good, or excellent. Seventy-one percent of participants agreed that their family life had improved. Sixty-two percent of the children reported that they had greatly improved their math skills.

Beyond these statistics, though, participants also noted some cultural shifts in their congregations. First, a leader of one of the programs noted that volunteering was becoming a new and significant part of the congregational culture:

> The people from the church who were helping in the kitchen were replacing themselves when they couldn't be here. They were calling other people from the church and saying, "Look, I can't be here this night, and they really need somebody to do this. Can you do it?" Which was really cool.

The idea of a cultural shift permeated many of the interviews:

> There isn't the big, strong expectation that people will make [congregational] programs a priority. But I think we may be at a place where we're starting to identify this as a culture shift that we need

to make, and I think that people—I don't want to get too excited about this—but I think that people are seeing what could be in the community.

Church participants also appreciated the inter-congregational partnerships that emerged from the process. Pastors reported that they now knew each other in ways that refuted some of their stereotypes and assumptions. Some resource-rich congregations supported other churches. In one instance, a neighboring church allowed another to use its facilities, even though it involved reduced rental revenues. "I would say that [the neighboring church] letting us use the building all the time is a big resource," said one church participant, "because [otherwise] they rent the church out."

CONCLUSION

Overall, one of the most compelling themes that emerged from the Family Leadership Initiative was that congregations were pleasantly surprised to see how much good they could actually accomplish in their neighborhoods. Competition, differing cultures, and varied leadership structures sometimes make congregational networking difficult. But when congregations do cooperate, they can be more efficient and more effective. They find that they can better carry out their own mission when they partner with neighboring churches.

Communities
of Caring

8

WHAT HAVE WE LEARNED?

We began this book by asking these questions: How hard is it to be a good neighbor? What does it mean not just for us as individuals, but also for us as a church, to be good neighbors to our community? In the chapters that followed, we've attempted to think together about how social science might help churches become better neighbors by making them more aware of themselves and more aware of those who live around them. This book has argued that when churches better understand who they are and what their neighborhoods are like, they can more effectively become good neighbors.

To that end, churches should realize first that caring for their communities, being good neighbors, comes from the very heart of their mission as churches. Regardless of context, caring for the local community is simply a matter of the church doing the business of the church.

Second, however, we saw that what a church has to offer is not the same as a professional social service agency. The church has many resources, among them a physical, stable presence in a neighborhood and many dedicated volunteers. Churches can also learn to understand and speak to the deep structural foundations of poverty. But they cannot replace professional social service agencies.

Third, we learned that city churches face particular, limiting challenges. They must learn to build "bridging ties" to their neighborhood rather than focusing all their attention on internal "binding ties." They must adapt to the needs of the residents in a changing neighborhood. They must understand and respond to the structural foundations of poverty.

In the face of these limitations and challenges, we looked in chapter 5 at ways churches might assess their resources and capacities with fresh eyes. In chapter 6, we looked at adding concern for systemic issues in our neighborhoods to our more well-developed concern over individual issues. In chapter 7, we expanded our vision of being good neighbors by looking at how cooperation among churches can multiply good work.

NEW CHALLENGES IN A CHANGING
URBAN ENVIRONMENT

As we move deeper into the twenty-first century, we need to keep in mind the shifting nature of cities and suburbs. As we have seen, almost all congregations want to be involved in their communities. However, the complexity of socio-economic issues makes wading into the pool of social service and social engagement risky activities for churches. Recent research has shown that poverty has been pushed into older, inner ring suburbs. At the same time, some formerly forgotten city neighborhoods have become targets of investment and gentrification. The oft-told story of "rich suburbs, poor city" no longer has the same resonance. Will churches be able to discern and respond to these changes? Will they be able to identify the intersection of the community's needs and the congregation's strengths and assets?

Most churches are concerned about engaging their communities well. The strong sales of books like *Toxic Charity: How Churches and Charities Hurt Those They Help* and *When Helping Hurts: How to Alleviate Poverty Without Hurting the Poor … and Yourself* reveal just how thoughtful congregations would like to be with their social engagement. Congregations clearly want to think more explicitly and intentionally about how they might most effectively engage their communities. Some even see local engagement as a badge of status.

However, I have reservations about any systems or steps that can be uniformly presented to *all* congregations. In fact, churches remain highly context-specific. By that I mean that churches reside in particular places, cultures, built environments, natural environments, and social settings that make universal translation pretty difficult. The path for nurturing a racially integrated congregation in Los Angeles or New York might not translate to Grand Rapids or Omaha. Community engagement also remains sensitive to the particularities of location. However, we can say this: congregational engagement cannot be *just* about building relationships. Such a notion downplays the significant systemic factors that keep poverty in place. How much power do we think our relationships have? Enough on their own to change a market-based economy that limits public transportation and full-time, well-paying jobs?

CARING COMMUNITIES

At the same time, it is helpful for congregations to realize that they are not social service agencies. In fact, recognizing their limits might allow them to better understand how they can most effectively serve their communities. One sociologist has suggested that churches should not identify themselves as service providers similar to the Red Cross or welfare department. Instead, they should think of themselves as "caring communities."

Caring communities differ from social service agencies in three primary ways. First, social interaction in caring communities takes place more regularly and over longer periods of time. This interaction includes a wide variety of activities, from worship to meetings to meals to softball to yard work. Second, social service providers tend to define relationships in ways that are unfamiliar in caring communities. For instance, terms typically used in social service relationships include "providers," "recipients," and "clients." Caring communities talk about friends and partners, spouses and children, young and old. Third, relationships in caring communities are what social scientists call "thick" relationships. They involve a "set of shared values, beliefs, understandings, traditions, and norms." On the other hand, the relationships between service organizations and clients can be described as "thin." They are defined as contracts, and they operate at an "arms-length" rather than being warm and personal.

The notion of a caring community affirms the historic strengths of congregations. Churches tend to be places where friendships are nurtured. Caring for those in need is emphasized. Small groups encourage participants to be attentive to one another. All these are important aspects of a caring community.

NURTURING A SENSE OF SOLIDARITY

However, congregations should also consider the larger implications of justice. Such a reorientation may cause them to engage issues of poverty in different ways. Moreover, if churches fail to understand the factors that cause rampant poverty, they may become complicit in the very systems that perpetuate the grinding despair of social inequality in the United States. Perhaps congregations should not just meet the material needs of the poor. Perhaps they should also become public witnesses to systems of injustice. In short, more complex understandings of poverty might encourage congregations to more effectively stand with the poor in their neighborhood. This is another way to be a caring community.

As we discussed earlier, poverty has complex roots. Yet the evidence from social science is quite clear that simply modifying lifestyles is not enough to overcome poverty. Mentoring and other relationships may help some. But those efforts don't necessarily overcome substandard education, inadequate housing, a dearth of jobs that pay a living wage, exorbitant health care costs, or lack of access to reliable transportation. If congregations say, "Yes, we want to help those in need around us," they cannot close their eyes to the systems of inequality that cause the need. If they do close their eyes and also become mute, their silence makes them complicit with these very conditions. In other words, to not question the systems that cause such deep inequalities, to allow the status quo to hum along unquestioned, functions as a form of quiet support.

One theologian has argued that when a congregation begins to serve the poor in its local neighborhood, it has already entered "into solidarity" with those who have been marginalized by the larger society. That solidarity demands more than just meeting a few identified material needs. Rather, it requires that the church, especially deacons, *speak* in opposition to "the social, political, and economic institutions and conditions under which the material need has arisen in the first place." In other words, actions *don't* always speak for themselves. "Those in the diaconate must not only give a fish to the hungry, or even be prepared to teach a hungry person to fish, but *also* intelligently sound the alarm to Church and society when the fish are dying due to human pollutants and political neglect."

A resident of a core city neighborhood offered a good example of putting such a strategy into action.

> When you have a church and drug dealers are selling drugs on its corner, the church needs to pull its congregation together, and they need to think about an active way to develop a plan of action that solves the problem. That means attacking the issue on a political front, like writing or protesting. It means doing whatever they can on an economic front to empower people so that they don't have to sell drugs. It may mean standing on the corner all night to prevent people from doing it. You can't say that it's wrong for people to sell drugs and not challenge them. Any organization that believes in God can never, never, under any circumstances justify their inaction with regard to social injustice.

In other words, if churches really care about their communities, they must act in multiple ways. Yes, they should build relationships. Yes, they should offer programs. Yes, they should speak about unjust practices. Yes, they should look for ways to make their communities safer and better for everyone who lives there. Congregations can build relationships *and* be encouraged to consider their influence regarding systems. They can play a role by using their status to focus on creating better laws, improved public transportation, fairer court systems, and improved walkability in their neighborhoods.

BUILDING ON A HISTORY OF CARING

If our churches become good neighbors, we will be continuing a long Christian tradition. The radical charity of early Christians set them apart as a faith community in the Roman Empire. Churches took seriously Chrysostom's challenge to avoid "foolishness and public madness" by actively caring for their neighbors. As a young religion, it was the Christian practices of community engagement, especially feeding the poor and ministering to the sick, that struck onlookers as so attractively revolutionary that they became converts. Even before Chrysostom uttered his inspirational words, the Roman emperor Julian the Apostate became so jealous of these winsome deeds that he ordered his cult priests to mimic the Christian acts of charity.

As churches engage with their communities, it should hearten us to remember the sweepingly generous charity of the historic Christian church. Early Christians likely deliberated very little about who was deserving and who failed to measure up. Moreover, they simply assumed that as they gave aid to those who asked, they gave aid to Christ himself. Churches today should likewise not be afraid to generously love their community.

Jesus told us to love God and to love our neighbors as ourselves (Luke 10:25-28). He told us in the story of the good Samaritan that our neighbors include those who live next to our families and our churches, including people who are very different from the congregation. To be neighborly is sometimes hard. We need to pick people up from the side of the road, but we also need to provide safe roads where they can travel securely and safe inns where they can stay. To love our neighbor is to love our neighborhood and to make better places and more just systems for everyone.

Although its familiarity has likely sanded down the edges of this command, churches should remember that loving our neighbor is a radical decision. It requires—perhaps counterintuitively—more than creating relationships. It also demands addressing the *systems* and the *places* people inhabit.

I hope that congregations feel encouraged to build on the good work they have begun. Churches should continue to care for individuals *and* address the systems that influence people's lives. God has given these caring communities the gifts that will bring relief to local neighbors and neighborhoods *and* help them to flourish. God empowers congregations to do the good work of Christ's church.

Notes

Stories in each chapter may use aliases to protect the identity of people and places.

Series Editor's Foreword

9 Midway along the journey of our life: the opening verse of *The Inferno* by Dante Alighieri, trans. Mark Musa (Bloomington and Indianapolis: Indiana University Press, 1995), 19.

10 We are always on the road: from Calvin's 34th sermon on Deuteronomy (5:12-14), preached on June 20, 1555 (*Ioannis Calvini Opera quae supersunt Omnia*, ed. Johann-Wilhelm Baum et al. [Brunsvigae: C.A. Schwetschke et Filium, 1883], 26.291), as quoted by Herman Selderhuis (*John Calvin: A Pilgrim's Life* [Downers Grove, IL: InterVarsity, 2009], 34).

10 a gift of divine kindness: from the last chapter of Calvin's French version of the *Institutes of the Christian Religion*. Titled "Of the Christian Life," the entire chapter is a guide to wise and faithful living in this world (*John Calvin, Institutes of the Christian Religion, 1541 French Edition*, trans. Elsie Anne McKee [Grand Rapids: Eerdmans, 2009], 704).

Chapter 1

16 Later leaders like John Chrysostom: For a quick history of John Chrysostom, see Robert A. Krupp, "Golden Tongue and

Iron Will," *Christian History* 44 (1994), https://christianhistory institute.org/magazine/article/golden-tongue-and-iron-will.

19 In fact, a neighborhood has so much influence: Joe Cortright and Dillon Mahmoudi, "Lost in Place: Why the Persistence and Spread of Concentrated Poverty—Not Gentrification—Is Our Biggest Urban Challenge," *City Observatory* (December 2014), http://cityobservatory.org/lost-in-place/.

Chapter 2

23 A case from Wisconsin: Ellen Gabler, "Mayor Tom Barret Appeals to Churches on 12th Ceasefire Sabbath," *The Milwaukee Journal Sentinel* (May 15, 2016), http://www.jsonline.com /news/milwaukee/mayor-tom-barrett-appeals-to-churches-to -help-stem-violence-on-12th-ceasefire-sabbath-b99725646z1 -379582141.html.

25 Elizabeth Dias: See journalist Elizabeth Dias' insightful story on Latino Protestants: "Evangélicos!" *Time* (April 15, 2013): 20-28. For more detail on the social and civic engagement of Latino Protestant congregations, see chapter 6 in Mark T. Mulder, Aida I. Ramos, and Gerardo Martí, *Latino Protestants in America* (Lanham, MD: Rowman & Littlefield, 2017).

26 Recent surveys report: For more detail on overall disillusionment with the ability of congregations solve social problems, see Michael Lipka, "Are Churches Key to Solving Social Problems? Fewer Americans Now Think So," Pew Research Center (July 18, 2016), http://www.pewresearch.org/ fact-tank/2016/07/18/are-churches-key-to-solving-social-problems-fewer-americans-now-think-so/.

27 We might even say that receiving aid: Ram A. Cnaan, *The Invisible Caring Hand: American Congregations and the Provision of Welfare* (New York: New York University Press, 2002), 115.

27 Individuals who attend churches: Edward C. Polson, "Putting Civic Participation in Context: Examining the Effects of Congregational Structure and Culture," *Review of Religious Research* 58 (2016): 75-100, p. 97, and Kraig Beyerlein and John R. Hipp, "From Pews to Participation: The Effect of Congregation Activity and Context on Bridging Civic Engagement," *Social Problems* 53, no. 1 (2006): 97-117.

28 One study found: Robert D. Putnam and David E. Campbell, *American Grace: How Religion Divides and Unites Us* (New York: Simon and Schuster, 2010).

Chapter 3

33 On a rainy Sunday morning: For more detail on the social and civic engagement of Latino Protestant congregations, see chapter 6 in Mark T. Mulder, Aida Ramos, and Gerardo Martí, *Latino Protestants in America.*

34 Congregations also possess certain features: For more on congregational life, see Nancy Ammerman, *Pillars of Faith: American Congregations and Their Partners* (Berkeley: University of California Press, 2005), and Nancy Ammerman, *Congregation and Community* (New Brunswick, NJ: Rutgers University Press, 1997).

35 For example, a recent twenty-five-year study in Baltimore: Karl Alexander, Doris Entwistle, and Linda Olson, *The Long Shadow: Family Background, Disadvantaged Urban Youth, and the Transition to Adulthood* (New York: Russell Sage Foundation, 2014).

36 Another recent book about the South Side of Chicago: While she neglects to discuss the key role of congregations in city neighborhoods, Natalie Y. Moore offers an insightful introduction to the devastating effects of residential segregation in *South Side: A Portrait of Chicago and American Segregation* (New York: St. Martin's Press, 2016).

36 **But others have actively helped their communities restruc-
ture:** Paul D. Numrich and Elfriede Wedam, *Religion and
Community in the New Urban America* (New York: Oxford
University Press, 2015), 7.

36 **Unfortunately, researchers often underestimate:** Numrich
and Wedam, *Religion and Community*, 2.

37 **These churches remain:** Meredith Ramsay, "Redeeming
the City: Exploring the Relationship Between Church and
Metropolis, *Urban Affairs Review* 33, no. 5 (1998): 598.

37 **For instance, a 2006 study of 1,400 Philadelphia congre-
gations:** Ram A. Cnaan, Stephanie C. Bodde, Charlene C.
McGrew, and Jennifer J. Kang, *The Other Philadelphia Story:
How Local Congregations Support Quality of Life in Urban
America* (Philadelphia: University of Pennsylvania Press,
2006).

37 **A similar study in Kent County**: Edwin Hernandez and Neil
Carlson, *Gatherings of Hope: How Congregations Contribute
to the Quality of Life in Kent County* (Grand Rapids: Calvin
College Center for Social Research, 2008).

39 **In other words, these interviews revealed**: Cnaan, *The Invisible Caring Hand*, 19.

39 **A Canadian study reported:** Mike Wood Daly, "The Halo
Project: Valuing Toronto's Faith Congregations," Cardus (June
2016), http://www.haloproject.ca/phase-1-toronto.

41 **Recent studies also indicate**: William Frey, "Demo-
graphic Reversal: Cities Thrive, Suburbs Sputter," *Brookings*,
June 29, 2012. https://www.brookings.edu/opinions/
demographic-reversal-cities-thrive-suburbs-sputter/.

41 **Moreover, some scholars have asserted that some religious
traditions**: James Bielo, "City of Man, City of God: The
Re-Urbanization of American Evangelicals," *City and Society*

23, no. 1 (2011): 2-23. See also Wes Markofski, *New Monasticism and the Transformation of American Evangelicalism* (New York: Oxford University Press, 2015).

Chapter 4

46 In the words of political scientists: Robert D. Putnam, *Bowling Alone: The Collapse and Revival of American Community* (New York: Touchstone Books, 2001).

46 A study of congregations in a district of Boston: Omar McRoberts, *Streets of Glory: Church and Community in a Black Urban Neighborhood* (Chicago: University of Chicago Press, 2003), 135.

47 The author of this study: McRoberts, *Streets of Glory*, 128.

48 In fact, research has shown that churches: Bill Bishop, *The Big Sort: How the Clustering of Like-Minded America is Tearing Us Apart* (New York: Houghton Mifflin, 2008).

50 A recent study reported that certain Christians in America: Julie Zauzmer, "Christians Are More Than Twice as Likely to Blame a Person's Poverty On Lack of Effort," *The Washington Post*, August 3, 2017. https://www.washingtonpost.com/news/acts-of-faith/wp/2017/08/03/christians-are-more-than-twice-as-likely-to-blame-a-persons-poverty-on-lack-of-effort/?utm_term=.6fbb3db8a726.

54 Those lifestyles are passed down: For succinct yet thorough discussion of the history and staying power of the "culture of poverty" thesis, see Susan D. Greenbaum, *Blaming the Poor: The Long Shadow of the Moynihan Report on Cruel Images About Poverty* (New Brunswick, NJ: Rutgers University Press, 2015).

55 They will need to reconsider: Sandra L. Barnes, *The Cost of Being Poor: A Comparative Study of Life in Poor Urban Neighborhoods in Gary, Indiana* (New York: State University of New York Press, 2005).

56 However, recent research on city churches: See Mark T. Mulder and Amy Jonason, "White Evangelical Congregations in Cities and Suburbs: Social Engagement, Geography, Diffusion, and Social Disembeddedness," *City and Society* 29, no. 1 (2017): 104-26.

57 One recent study found: Omri Elisha, *Moral Ambition: Mobilization and Social Outreach in Evangelical Megachurches* (Berkeley: University of California Press, 2011), 183.

58 But it remains one of many activities: Mark Chaves, *Congregations in America* (Cambridge, MA: Harvard University Press, 2004), 93.

Chapter 5

61 If churches should not replace public social service agencies: See Numrich and Wedam, *Religion and Community in the New Urban America.*

61 For instance, one study found: Nancy T. Kinney and William E. Winter, "Places of Worship and Neighborhood Stability," *Journal of Urban Affairs* 28, no. 4 (2006).

62 For instance, one Canadian study: Daly, "The Halo Project."

64 When the congregation and the broader community collaborate: See William McKinney, Anthony T. Ruger, Diane Cohen, and Robert Jeager, "Resources," in Nancy T. Ammerman, Jackson W. Carroll, Carl S. Dudley, and William McKinney, eds., *Studying Congregations: A New Handbook* (Nashville, TN: Abingdon Press, 1998), 132-166; quote at 158.

64 The erosion of community ties: See Putnam, *Bowling Alone.*

65 And they can offer reinforcement and support: Robert Wuthnow, *Saving America? Faith-Based Services and the Future of Civil Society* (Princeton: Princeton University Press, 2004), 63.

65 Have you ever wondered: Wuthnow, *Saving America*, 62.

66 Almost every religious tradition: Ram A. Cnaan and Daniel W. Curtis, "Religious Congregations as Voluntary Associations: An Overview," *Nonprofit and Voluntary Sector Quarterly,* 42, no. 1 (2012): 1-27, at 16.

67 Sociologist Nancy Ammerman has argued: Ammerman, *Pillars of Faith.*

68 Other social scientists argue that congregations: Cnaan, *The Invisible Caring* Hand, 255.

68 Congregations have many resources: McKinney and others, *Studying Congregations,* 132.

Chapter 6

71 James Robertson, a fifty-six-year-old Detroiter: For more on Robertson and his commute, see Bill Laitner, "Heart and Soul: Detroiter Walks 21 Miles in Work Commute," *Detroit Free Press,* January 31, 2015. https://www.freep.com/story/news /local/michigan/oakland/2015/01/31/detroit-commuting-troy -rochester-hills-smart-ddot-ubs-banker-woodward-buses -transit/22660785/.

72 For instance, the Sisters of St. Casimir: Numrich and Wedam, *Religion and Community*, 80-81.

72 Some inner-city churches are large, established congregations: Robert Wuthnow, *Loose Connections: Joining Together in America's Fragmented Communities* (Cambridge, MA: Harvard University Press, 1998), 124.

73 Research indicates that some core cities: Alan Ehrenhalt, *The Great Inversion and the Future of the American City* (New York: Knopf, 2012).

73 Stories in *The New York Times*: Ben Austen, "The Post-Post-Apocalyptic Detroit," *The New York Times Magazine,* July 11, 2014, http://www.nytimes.com/2014/07/13/magazine/the -post-post-apocalyptic-detroit.html?_r=2.

75 Although gentrification should not be overlooked: While not dismissing or making light of the profound consequences of gentrification, Joe Cortright and Dillon Mahmoudi offer a rich analysis of poverty's strengthening death grip on certain urban neighborhoods in "Lost in Place: Why the Persistence and Spread of Concentrated Poverty—Not Gentrification—Is Our Biggest Urban Challenge," City Observatory (December 2014), http://cityobservatory.org/lost-in-place/.

75 High poverty neighborhoods: Cortright and Mahmoudi, "Lost in Place."

76 A 1984 study of Hartford, Connecticut: David Roozen, William McKinney, and Jackson W. Carroll, *Varieties of Religious Presence: Mission in Public Life* (New York: Pilgrim Press, 1984).

Chapter 7

83 This resistance to cooperation: R. Stephen Warner, "The Place of the Congregation in the Contemporary Religious Configuration," in *American Congregations, Volume 2: New Perspectives in the Study of Congregations*, ed. James P. Wind and James W. Lewis (Chicago: University of Chicago Press, 1994).

84 Rather, the Kent County study: Hernandez and Carlson, *Gatherings of Hope*, v.

84 Congregations working together: In a somewhat stunning argument, the former mayor of Albuquerque makes this case in a *policy* book about the important role that churches can play as cities and suburbs think about coordinating and working together. See David Rusk, *Inside Game/Outside Game: Winning Strategies for Saving Urban America* (Washington DC: Brookings Institution Press, 2001), 333.

85 In his 2008 book: Bill Bishop, *The Big Sort: Why the Clustering of Like-Minded America is Tearing Us Apart* (New York: Houghton Mifflin, 2008).

85 Indeed, University of Maryland political scientist: Quoted in Bishop, *The Big Sort*, 180.

85 Bishop also describes: Bishop, *The Big Sort*, 180.

85 One attender told some sociologists: Michael Emerson and Christian Smith, *Divided by Faith: Evangelical Religion and the Problem of Race in America* (New York: Oxford University Press, 2000), 122.

86 Challenges by congregational leaders: For more on how congregations demonstrate local engagement and yet avoid local issues in worship, see Mark T. Mulder, "Worshipping to Stay the Same: Avoiding the Local to Maintain Solidarity," in *Christians and the Color Line: Race and Religion After* Divided by Faith, ed. J. Russell Hawkins and Philip Luke Sinitiere (New York: Oxford University Press, 2014).

86 If a congregation does nothing: Wuthnow, *Saving America*, 62.

86 One study of Chicago's neighborhoods: Robert J. Sampson, *Great American City: Chicago and the Enduring Neighborhood Effect* (Chicago: The University of Chicago Press, 2012), 205.

87 The resulting dynamic is a mismatch: Sampson, *Great American City*, 204-205

87 Denominational resources and loyalty have declined: Wuthnow, *Loose Connections*, 215.

91 I would say that [the neighboring church]: See Mark T. Mulder, Kristen Napp, Neil E. Carlson, Zig Ingraffia, Khary Bridgewater, and Edwin Hernandez, "The Role of the Congregation in Community Service: A Philanthropic Case Study," *The Foundation Review* 4, no. 3 (2012): 21-41.

Chapter 8

97 However, I have reservations: To read more about how church diversity "experts" may actually confuse racial issues for congregations, see Gerardo Martí and Michael O. Emerson, "The Rise of the Diversity Expert: How American Evangelicals Simultaneously Accentuate and Ignore Race," in *The New Evangelical Social Engagement*, ed. Brian Steensland and Philip Goff (New York: Oxford University Press, 2014).

98 **How much power:** For some provocative thoughts on churches, relationships, poverty, and systems, see John Thornton, "The Inadequacy of the Transforming Power of Relationships," *Medium*, December 21, 2017. https://medium .com/@johnthorntonjr/the-inadequacy-of-the-transforming -power-of-relationships-a4bebec34c76.

98 **One sociologist has suggested:** Wuthnow, *Saving America*, 64.

98 **Caring communities differ from social service agencies:** Wuthnow, *Saving America*, 65.

100 **If congregations say:** Theologian David Guretzki leans heavily on Karl Barth in his discussion of the proper role for the diaconate, "Deacons, Church, and World: Deacons Should Be Permitted to Look Deeper at the Roots of the Social Issues Causing Material Need," *Comment* (October 9, 2014). https:// www.cardus.ca/comment/article/4322/deacons-church-and -world/.

100 **One theologian has argued:** Guretzki, "Deacons, Church, and World."

101 **When you have a church and drug dealers are selling drugs on its corner:** Wuthnow, *Loose Connections*, 215-16.

102 **As a young religion:** Jeremy Beer, *The Philanthropic Revolution: An Alternative History of American Charity* (Phil- adelphia: The University of Pennsylvania Press, 2015), 25.